Management
Insights

Discovering the Truths to Management Success

Ken Carnes, David Cottrell and Mark C. Layton

CornerStone
Leadership Institute

www.**cornerstoneleadership**.com

CornerStone
Leadership Institute

insight

\ ĭn′ sīt' \ *noun*

1 : The capacity to discern the nature of a situation;
2 : The act or result of apprehending the inner
   nature of things or of seeing intuitively.

– American Heritage Dictionary

Management Insights

Printed in the United States of America
ISBN: 0-9719424-8-X

Credits
Editor   Alice Adams
Contributing Editor   Juli Baldwin, The Baldwin Group, Dallas, TX
Design, art direction, and production   Back Porch Creative, Plano, TX

Contents

The Problem...

The High Cost of
Management Failure

An estimated 40% of all managers fail within their first 18 months on the job.

It's hard to believe, but it's true. According to studies by the Center for Creative Leadership and Manchester Partners International, almost half of all new management hires will fail. But what exactly do these studies indicate? How do these managers "fail"? Do they not achieve their goals and objectives? Do they fail to meet senior management's expectations? Are they stalled in their progression up the corporate ladder?

Unfortunately, the answer is harsh. "Failure," as it's defined in these studies, means that, more than likely, new managers will no longer be in their position after 18 months. They will either be demoted, terminated, "voluntarily" resign, or perform significantly below expectations. That makes the findings even more dramatic!

And what about the other 60% of managers? Does the fact that they don't fail mean they're successful? Not necessarily. Not failing doesn't equal success. A manager can still have his or her job and yet not be considered successful. The truth is that only a small percentage of leaders exceed upper management's expectations.

Management failure can be found in virtually all businesses – large and small, service and manufacturing, profit and non-profit. And the consequences of management failure are enormous.

Leadership failure is one of the top two reasons for overall business failure.

That alone should make us sit up and take notice. But there's more. Management failure is also the number one reason for turnover in organizations. Obviously, finding and developing the right people for management is crucial to long-term organizational success.

Management failure costs corporations billions of dollars each year. It is a cost that can't be "written off" and probably doesn't have a specific line item or cost center to charge. Although you can calculate the cost of hiring and re-training a new manager, the largest expenses can't easily be accounted for. It's difficult to put a dollar amount on the cost of rebuilding a team, employee turnover, poor morale, low productivity, conflict, legal issues, and lost opportunities.

But there are huge costs to the individual as well. Often these "failed managers" have invested years in their careers. Many have worked all their lives for an opportunity to manage others. Consequently, their failures have a dramatic impact on their self-esteem, confidence, and even their future success.

If people strive for years to break into management and make personal sacrifices to earn subsequent management promotions, why so many failures?

Could it be these managers are incompetent? Are those doing the hiring allowing people who don't have the required technical skills to be placed in such important roles? Sure, the wrong person is occasionally hired for a management position. However, incompetence accounts for only a small percentage of management failures. Most new managers have the technical skills necessary to be successful. In fact, when the best salesperson, nurse, teacher, engineer, production worker, etc., is promoted into management, it's often because they've excelled in the technical aspects of their jobs.

Is it possible managers don't have the desire to become excellent leaders? Maybe. But in reality, most managers attack their jobs with energy and enthusiasm, wanting to be the very best. New managers – both experienced and inexperienced – will usually do whatever they think is necessary to be successful.

So if new managers have both the competency and the desire to become great leaders, why do so many of them fail so fast?

We believe the root of this problem is a lack of knowledge and understanding about how to lead others.

Effective management skills are completely different from the skills required to excel in sales, nursing, teaching, engineering or production. Just because someone is a stellar individual contributor doesn't mean they can successfully lead people. That is a fact many people in business have never understood. There's no guarantee the star salesperson will become an effective sales manager, the best teacher will make the best principal, the outstanding nurse will make a great supervisor, or the most productive worker will become the best team leader.

The best individual contributors *can* make excellent managers...if they are prepared for their new management role. But all too often, people are promoted without really knowing what they're getting into and without much training on how to lead other people. The good news is that management skills can be learned, just as sales techniques, nursing skills, or engineering methods can be learned.

Unfortunately, failure is not limited to those who are brand new to the management ranks. Even experienced managers fail at an alarming rate when placed in new situations. Leaders are constantly being promoted to take over new teams, divisions, and projects. Managers accept positions in new companies and new industries. Any time a manager changes positions, even within the management ranks, the process of being a "new" manager starts all over again.

Every step up the corporate ladder puts a manager into an unfamiliar leadership situation. The strategies that brought a manager previous successes may not be enough to ensure continued success. Tactics that worked with one team won't work with other teams. Each new situation requires more knowledge and new skills. And because these "new" managers are "experienced," they receive even less training than those who are new to management.

Actually, with all the challenges new managers face, it's somewhat surprising the failure rate isn't higher!

Management Insights will provide you with the knowledge and understanding critical to your success as a manager. First, we'll go behind the management curtain and unveil the truths about a manager's role. We'll take an in-depth look at common management myths – those incorrect, preconceived notions about management – and discover what it's really like to be a successful manager.

We'll help you overcome the obstacles to management success by dealing directly with the key reasons why managers fail. More importantly, you'll learn specifically what you can do to avoid the same pitfalls. You'll find strategies, techniques and tools you can use to successfully lead others.

Finally, you'll have access to the experiences of highly successful managers who have gone before you. You'll benefit from a number of "Personal Insights" – words of wisdom from top-level managers in some of the most respected companies in the country.

When you decided to pursue a career in management, you chose a wonderful and challenging profession. You have the opportunity to make a positive impact on the lives of others. The rewards are tremendous... if you are prepared for the challenges. This book was written to help you meet and overcome those challenges.

Whether you've been in management for years, you're a brand new manager, or you're thinking about a management position with another company, you'll find insights in this book that will help you be a better leader.

If you will take the information and apply it, you will dramatically reduce the likelihood of failure. But more importantly, you'll have a framework for lasting success.

Management Insights will show you the true nature of management success and pave the way for you to become the manager you've always wanted to be.

Management Success...

What It Looks Like

Without question, the attributes separating successful managers from those who fail are often elusive. Many management gurus have attempted to write about what makes a leader successful. Yet their theories often fail to provide a cookie-cutter recipe for success…and with good reason. A successful manager's approach often depends on variables such as the task at hand, the make-up of the team, and the needs of individual team members. However, even when these variables are taken into consideration, a successful manager shares many attributes with other successful managers.

Think about both the good and poor managers you've worked for in the past. How were they alike? How were they different? What traits did the good managers have in common?

Truly effective managers have all the "right stuff" to move their teams to higher levels with relative ease. Poor managers don't move teams higher. But interestingly, they go through the same motions as successful managers: working with team members, going to meetings, communicating, creating reports, solving problems, etc. Great managers make the job look easy. But so do poor managers. So what's the difference?

Successful managers deliver bottom-line results to the organization by developing other people.

Your role as a manager is to deliver results. And yet, just because you're getting results doesn't mean you're successful. If you're having to do all the work yourself to achieve those results, you're just faking success. You must accomplish results and get work done through other people. Your success as a manager will be reflected in the results of your team.

Excellent managers realize much is expected of them; but they also know they can only accomplish great things with the help of others. They understand they must influence people's attitudes, aspirations, emotions and drive – people who, at any given point, may or may not produce, depending on the circumstances. Successful managers are effective at making things happen for other people, not just for themselves, and they derive fulfillment from the success of others.

Although the techniques they use may vary based on the circumstances, effective managers deliver results by:

+ Developing a common vision;

+ Influencing people to give their best;

+ Motivating and building high-performance teams;

+ Breaking down individual and organizational barriers,

+ Stimulating and promoting innovation; and

+ Creating energy and cultivating enthusiasm.

If you achieve the goals of delivering bottom-line results for the company and positively influencing the careers of the people you manage, it will be because you've also succeeded at the very reason many professionals become managers – because they think they can do the job better than it's ever been done before.

Now that we understand what it means to be a successful manager, let's uncover the obstacles that could prevent you from achieving that success...

"Management's goal should be to do everything in their power to help others be as successful as possible. Management succeeds only when the rest of the organization succeeds."

– Unknown

Management Myths...

And The Realities Behind Them

W e've all heard management "truisms" during our years in the workplace. Many are as old as dirt itself; so they must be true, right?

The answer to that question is a definite, "Ummm…not always!"

Indeed, there are many management myths that twirl like dervishes around the workplace. These traditions, stories and beliefs about what it's really like to be a manager have existed for years, and we've all "grown up" with them. They've been reinforced and passed down for so long that many people accept them as truth. But, as with other myths, management myths are false.

Many of these myths emerged from real-life experiences and may have been true in the past. But as the nature of business has changed, the concepts simply don't hold true anymore. The modern business environment is so dynamic that as new management trends and strategies emerge, many long-standing truths dissolve into myths and legends.

Some myths get started on college campuses where professors with little or no real-world management experience teach students about the "real" world of management.

Other management myths are innocent, albeit inaccurate, perceptions of life in the management ranks by those on the other side – the individual contributors who believe the grass is always greener on the other side of the desk. When viewed from the other side, what managers do looks easy and more rewarding than performing in an individual contributor role.

Although we might think these myths are harmless, they are actually key sources of misinformation and confusion. New managers often walk into their positions with a set of preconceived notions that are, in most cases, completely wrong! If you walk into a job expecting one thing, but the reality is something completely different, you limit your potential success before you even get started. You're already heading down a path toward failure and away from success.

These false notions about management affect even experienced managers. Often, people who have been in management for a while get "stuck" – maybe they haven't achieved the level of success they had hoped for. These managers know things aren't quite right, but they can't put their finger on what or where the problem is. Chances are, they're operating according to these management myths without even realizing it.

One of the keys to success as a leader is to objectively understand your position and role. To do that, you need to see these myths for what they are – unfounded and false ideas about manangement. In this section, we'll explore seven management myths, their assumptions, and why they are at odds with reality.

If you can debunk these myths and instead clearly see the day-to-day realities faced by managers, you stand a much greater chance of achieving the success you desire.

> *"The great enemy of the truth is very often not the lie – deliberate, contrived and dishonest; but the myth – persistent, persuasive and unrealistic."*
> – John F. Kennedy

Myth

"As a manager, I will have more freedom to do what I want to do."

Reality

You actually *lose* freedom when you become a manager – many of the freedoms you enjoyed as an individual contributor suddenly disappear.

Most people think managers have the freedom to schedule their time – a freedom many individual contributors do not have. Nothing could be further from the truth. As a manager, you actually have less freedom to choose how you spend your time. Why? Because you are now responsible for other people's time as well as your own; and this gargantuan task requires sacrifice…*yours*, to be exact! While you might control certain activities and schedules during the day, you now have so many additional responsibilities that your time is often scheduled for you. As a manager, the number of meetings you must attend increases dramatically – yet another activity you rarely have control over. On top of that, team members who need your help or insight snatch precious minutes between your scheduled "To Do's."

You also lose the freedom to schedule your out-of-office time. As an individual contributor, you probably had the freedom to take vacation whenever you wanted to, as long as there weren't several critical team members absent at the same time. But as a leader, you're held accountable for the entire team and their results. Who will be responsible for your team – and any problems that may arise – when you're not there? If even one team member is out, it's often not possible for the manager to also leave because someone has to cover the work. The truth is, it's harder, not easier, for managers to get away from the office.

Another freedom – like the freedom to complain about senior management decisions – also evaporates. When you become a manager, you also automatically become a role model, and **people are watching you closely every minute of every day**. Even if you don't agree with upper-management decisions, it is your job to make lemonade out of lemons – to make even the most unpopular decisions more palatable for your team. You cannot risk negativity among team members, no matter how you feel about the decisions you're asked to support.

Speaking of decisions, perhaps you thought that as a manager you would have the freedom to make more of your own decisions – decisions about processes, procedures, and systems. The reality is that your ability to make and implement decisions is limited by personnel, budget constraints, fixed resources, and conflicting priorities. Often you don't even have the freedom to hire the people you want and need for your team to be effective. Maybe there's a hiring freeze, or the best applicant wants more money than you can offer, or it's "strongly recommended" that you fill your position from within the company.

You can also expect to lose the freedom of having personal relationships at work. You cannot share your frustrations and fears with the people who follow your leadership. Nor can you freely share your innermost thoughts with team members – many of whom may have been your peers before you became a manager. When you accepted your management position, you also accepted the fact that **you can never NOT lead**. In short, your thoughts, actions and deeds follow you everywhere.

One of the great all-time management myths is that as a manager you can do what you want to do, when you want to do it. The reality is much different.

Greater responsibility usually means less freedom.

"As a manager, I will make more money."

Myth

Reality

Many new managers actually take a pay cut. Often, these pay reductions occur because most managers are not eligible for the overtime pay that non-exempt employees receive. In fact, many people who work a lot of overtime and many commissioned sales people out-earn their managers. Without a doubt, a promotion into management changes how you're paid. But this change may not translate into more money or fewer hours in the beginning.

Remember, as a manager you're expected to put in the hours necessary to produce results. That expectation boils down to coming in early, staying late, and possibly working weekends until the job is finished. According to one study, 80% of managers say they usually work overtime. Whereas the average American employee still works between 38 and 41 hours per week, the average manager works about 50 hours per week. But all this extra work is often done with little or no additional monetary compensation.

The good news is that managers who increase their teams' performance and productivity usually move up quickly. Even if you took a cut when you moved into management, your overall compensation (based on overall business results) will probably catch up with, and surpass, what you made as a team member.

People who think managers make "the big money" often don't see the trade-offs that come with that big money – things like more stress, additional responsibilities, being held accountable for other people's actions, having to answer to senior management, and being forced to make difficult decisions that affect people's lives. The truth is, being a manager does not mean making more money for the same number of hours and the same level of responsibility.

Even experienced managers fall victim to this myth. They accept promotions to run larger departments or take managerial positions within new companies – often with an increase in pay. But the same forces are at work in every management position. Every promotion naturally and automatically involves added responsibility and commitment. New jobs require more time up front to learn the business. As the old saying goes, you don't get something for nothing. It is rare indeed that you will make more money without having to give something more in return.

Certainly, there are some financial benefits to being in a management position. However, more often than not, those benefits are accompanied by greater responsibilities. With all that said, when you decided to move into management, you likely did so for the fulfillment that comes from making a difference and not for the money. Developing people and helping organizations grow are the passions of the most successful leaders.

**As a manager, you are compensated differently.
Initially, you may make less money
in exchange for added responsibility.**

Myth

"I am a good 'people person.'
People will naturally follow me."

Reality

You can be a good person who is well liked and still fail as a manager.

As a manager, you are not measured by how well you are liked and by how many people. We all want to be liked – that's only natural. We also want all of our thoughts, ideas and decisions to be readily accepted. But **management is NOT a popularity contest.** The stark reality is that "popular" rarely describes a good manager.

While your overall popularity is not important, it is important to earn the trust and respect of your people. The most effective managers *seem* to be popular and well liked because of the trust and respect shown them by the people they lead. Successful managers earn trust and respect by listening to their people, keeping the commitments they make, working hard to remove obstacles, and clearly communicating on a consistent basis.

Making difficult decisions and standing up for what you believe is right is not always easy and is often not well received by others in the organization. But you will gain the most respect and trust when you step up to the plate and make those difficult (and sometimes unpopular) decisions – like supporting your people in the face of controversy or "de-hiring" a well liked but ineffective employee. It is these challenging situations that define who you are as a manager and provide the foundation for long-term commitment from your team.

Many times you hear about managers who use consensus building to try and make everyone happy. There is a time and place for the consensus style of management; but every decision can't be "let's take a vote and go with the popular opinion." Effective managers have a knack for knowing when (and how) to involve the team in the decision-making process and when to make decisions alone.

Successful managers constantly communicate with their teams about the decision-making process itself and the thoughts and actions behind the decisions. This continuing education enables managers to make tough decisions and gain employee understanding and support, even when team members are not involved in the decision or when they disagree with the decision.

It is true that some people are naturally charismatic and may be perceived as a "born leader." But rest assured – no one is a born leader. You may undoubtedly have many of the characteristics of a leader; but **leadership must be earned**. Even if you have the charisma that draws people to you, you must take the time and effort to build trust, respect, and credibility with your team members if you want them to follow you long term.

It may surprise you to know that some of the most charismatic, people-oriented individual contributors fail when they become managers. Their need to be the center of attention and to be liked by everyone is a huge barrier to the requirement that, as a manager, they must be fair, consistent and objective in their dealings with people.

Management success is not based on how charismatic you are or how well your team likes you. Management success is based entirely on your ability to get others to accomplish goals. There are countless examples of highly successful leaders whose team members don't like them, but respect them nonetheless.

**People will follow you
only when you have earned
their trust and respect.**

Myth

"As a manager, I can make change happen more quickly and efficiently." (Translation: "If I were boss, things would be different around here.")

Reality

One of the principal reasons managers fail is because they try to make changes before they have earned the right to do so. In other words, they don't take the time to earn the trust of the people who will be responsible for implementing the change.

Think back to a time when you had a new manager who felt a burning need to make changes, initiate new processes, or revamp the existing culture. This manager probably believed that to have an immediate impact, he or she needed to show an action orientation. Perhaps the manager came to you and asked you to make a radical change in your daily routine. We've all been there – and wasn't our immediate reaction to mutter under our breath, "Who do they think they are...coming in and asking me to do things differently? They don't even know me or the situation around here."

Both first-time and experienced managers alike mistakenly think that in order to be successful, they must immediately change things when they are placed in a new situation. They wholeheartedly believe they can run things better than they were being run before. Whether they are new to management, new to the organization, or new to a particular team or department, these managers feel they must set a different course of action and make their mark quickly. They want to make a good impression and prove themselves worthy of their new position. And besides, upper management expects immediate change and immediate results, right?

The truth is that in most cases, senior management is not looking for fast, radical change. They're looking for sensible, sustainable change. They want a manager who can develop a high-performance team and be successful over the long haul – someone who will assess the situation, look at the options, and then make conscious change.

Effective change is not change just for the sake of change. It requires proper timing, communication, support and commitment. And it requires building trust and rapport. To create positive and lasting change, there must be a foundation of trust.

Remember, it's human nature to resist change – any change. Organizations are similar to the human body, and the individuals within these organizations are like the antibodies found in the human body. Antibodies attack and kill foreign organisms – regardless of whether the organisms are helpful or harmful. When a new manager introduces change (something foreign) into an organization, individuals (the antibodies) frequently attack the new idea and often kill it – regardless of whether the change is positive or negative.

Many times fresh perspectives, new ideas, and changes are absolutely needed within organizations. There may be processes or systems that don't work or situations that are detrimental to the success of the team and the organization. In fact, this is often the reason why a new manager is brought in – to fix the problems. But it's rare that a situation is so bad that it can't wait until you've earned some trust and respect before making changes.

One of the best pieces of advice we can give you as a manager in a new situation is to **not make radical changes during the first 90 days.** Certainly, taking action to fix the things that are "broken" or detrimental to achieving results is necessary. But other than addressing critical, immediate needs, a new manager should ask questions, listen carefully and observe for at least three months before changing protocols, processes or any other aspects of the business. Following this observation time, the manager can decide on a course of action for those things that must change.

When considering changes, even small ones, think about what impact the change will have once it's implemented. In many cases, a change that looks positive for one area of the business can create big problems in another. These problems can include increased costs, employee conflict within or between departments, and more work for other teams. Before making any change, consider whether the positive results achieved by the change could be overshadowed by negative repercussions. Wait until you have complete information before implementing new changes.

Great managers know that success doesn't come overnight. They realize they must take the time to build the trust, respect, understanding and buy-in necessary for powerful and lasting change.

Management is not about making changes for the sake of change. The timing of the change is just as important as the change itself.

"The most dangerous leadership myth is that leaders are born – that there is a genetic factor to leadership. This myth asserts that people simply either have certain charismatic qualities or not. That's nonsense; in fact, the opposite is true. Leaders are made rather than born."

– Warren G. Bennis

Myth

"I won't have to fire anyone...everybody's performance can be turned around."

Reality

There will be times when you, unfortunately, have to "de-hire" someone. This is, undoubtedly, the most difficult task a manager must face, but one that must be dealt with nevertheless.

As a manager, you will discover (if you haven't already) that there are three types of employees. Some are superstars – those individuals who have the experience, knowledge and motivation to be the best at their jobs. Others are "middle stars." They may not yet have the experience to be superstars; or perhaps they were superstars who burned out and lost their desire to be the best. And then there are the "falling stars." These are the people who do as little as they can get away with.

If you look at any given team, you can safely predict that 30% of the individuals will be superstars, 50% middle stars and 20% falling stars. As a manager, you'll have the opportunity to guide many people to improved performance. When you properly coach and reward each individual (regardless of what type of employee they are), most will develop and excel under your leadership – and that is exciting.

But some falling stars will not improve even with coaching. These individuals must be de-hired for their own good as well as that of the team. When managers ignore the performance problems of a few falling stars, the middle stars and superstars have to pick up the slack. You can bet these high performers won't stick around for long if their reward for good performance is more work.

What about the employee who is a superstar in some areas, but a falling star in others? In this case, the manager must decide if the individual's positive attributes outweigh the "baggage" that comes with them. Many times the baggage is that the employee is poisoning the work environment, alienating others on the team, or, even worse, alienating clients.

This type of individual – bringing the good, the bad and the ugly into the environment – may be a plus to the organization because their productivity greatly improves the team's overall performance. Yet, because of their toxic attitude, this productivity comes at a high price, and the employee becomes a long-term liability. Eventually, when the negatives begin to outweigh the positives, the effective manager is forced to fire this individual.

When management chooses to purge the organization of these toxic superstars, the remaining employees often rally around the team's goals and objectives. The net effect is that the team may actually do a better job collectively than they were doing when the top performer was still on board.

Finally, there will be situations – like workforce reduction decisions – when you may not have a say in the decision to de-hire team members. These decisions are passed down to you from upper management; and while you may not support them, these decisions must be carried out for the good of the organization.

Regardless of the reason, de-hiring someone is never easy – for them or for you. The person may never understand how or why they weren't meeting expectations. Often, the individual and his or her performance problems have survived numerous managers; so it may not be an issue of poor management. It may be the wrong person is in the job. It's often that simple, but it's a performance problem you have to address all the same.

De-hiring someone is also extremely hard on you. Your emotions will be involved; the employee's emotions will be involved; and the employee will probably not agree with you and may share some harsh words. Successful managers know they must be prepared when they have to face a de-hiring situation, and they seek the help of Human Resources.

The good news is that with the proper focus on good hiring techniques, the use of clear communication skills, and a commitment to providing ongoing coaching, the need for de-hiring is rare.

**Not all people are in the right jobs
at the right time for the right reasons.
Somewhere along the way,
you will have to de-hire someone.**

Myth

**"I will be successful because
I am in touch with my people."**

Reality

Success as a leader comes from developing a genuine connection with your people, not simply being in touch with them.

"Being in touch" represents a one-way flow of communication. Managers who are "in touch" often talk but don't listen; they ask for feedback and yet rarely follow up on it; they unexpectedly drop in to talk with a team member about a project without regard for that individual's time or other priorities.

On the other hand, connecting with team members involves establishing and maintaining a two-way flow of communication between manager and employee. While connecting with team members may sound easy, know that it takes time and effort. Just as a sturdy foundation will support a building for decades, establishing a strong connection with your team creates a firm foundation for long-term success.

New managers who don't take the time to connect with their teams are flirting with disaster. We hear story after story about managers who step into a new position and, without knowing anything about the team or its members, let everyone know "this is the way it's going to be." These managers believe that to be successful they must demonstrate up front who the boss is. Their approach alienates and de-motivates the team and inevitably turns the team against them. These managers are lucky if they last six months.

So how can you effectively connect with your team members and avoid potential problems? Take time out from busy schedules and deadlines to get together with each individual and really get to know them. Discover what they are passionate about, what motivates and drives them. Have them talk about both their strengths and weaknesses. The purpose of this time spent with your employees is for them to become real to you. But it's also an opportunity for you to become real to them – to share who you are and what drives and motivates you.

It's critical that you learn about the team's history – its successes and its challenges. Find out what team members see as the opportunities and obstacles that lie ahead. Listen intently, take notes, remember what they say – it is valuable information. Then, armed with this information, you can slowly evolve your own style of managing and motivating this unique team.

The most successful managers make connecting with team members a top priority, and they develop an intentional and consistent pattern of communication. Constantly calling ad hoc meetings, making impromptu phone calls and sending barrages of e-mails only cause confusion and frustration and actually create a disconnect with team members. The nature of today's complex and rapidly changing work environment makes connecting with team members even more difficult and yet all the more critical. As span of control continues to increase, team members may be located at home, across the country or across the globe. The successful manager develops unique and innovative ways to stay connected with team members despite these challenges.

Here are some other ways you can connect with your team:

♦ Look for and encourage fresh ideas from team members.

♦ Pitch in and help your team do some of the small things.

♦ Offer solutions to help solve problems.

♦ Show you care about employees by listening to them and acting on what you hear.

♦ Recognize successes.

♦ Focus time and attention on a person's strengths and those things they are passionate about rather than their weaknesses.

♦ Give each person your undivided attention when you're with them – no multitasking or cell phone calls.

Don't become what some call a "seagull manager" – one who flies in, looks around, eats the food, poops everywhere and flies away. Connect with your team. The more informed and knowledgeable you are about your people, the more effective and successful you will be. Make your interactions meaningful and ensure that you add value to every contact. If you can't connect with people, you can't develop people. And if you can't develop people, you won't be successful.

**Work to develop a genuine
and consistent connection
with each of your team members.**

"It's easy to get everyone on the team to work together."

Myth

Reality

There's nothing easy about management. Leading people is hard work. Leading sharp, talented, thinking employees is even more difficult.

One of the first things successful managers strive to do is get everyone "on the same page" – where everybody works together as a cohesive unit toward a common goal. This is certainly a worthy objective, but it takes time and concentrated effort to make it happen. You might think that it wouldn't be so hard…after all, everyone on the team has the same goals and objectives, right? Hardly! It's rare that every member of the team sings out of the same songbook, much less the same song. And if they do sing from the same page, you'll probably find that at least one person can't carry a tune.

Many leaders are shocked to discover just how difficult managing very diverse and complex individuals can be. The people on your team may or may not share your views, thoughts or desire to succeed. The team has goals, quotas or objectives, right? It's virtually guaranteed that your level of commitment to these goals is different than your team members' commitment. That doesn't make them bad employees. It's just that their priorities may be different than yours.

Let's say, for example, your team includes some 20-somethings right out of college, some 30-somethings, and some 40-somethings. Each person – because of where they are in their lives and careers – brings different talents and experiences to the team, along with different needs and priorities. Some have worked for 10 or 20 years and for several companies; others are rookies. There are hard-chargers, slow-starters, and "Steady Eddies." They come from diverse backgrounds with various personal situations. They have distinctive personalities and individual views. And (don't forget this – it's important) they all see you through separate sets of eyes and respond to your management style differently. In most cases, the only common trait shared by team members is that they are all on the same team, working for the same company.

Molding a productive team from a group of people who are different in every way is like taking mud and dirt and stones and wildflowers and creating a beautiful landscape. Team building is one of the toughest jobs a manager has because of the variables represented in the group. Yet this diversity is the very thing that creates the opportunity for extraordinary results. If your team members were all the same, your results would be constrained by the limited experiences your team shares.

There's a valuable lesson we can learn about team building from the world of sports. The most successful baseball coaches know that the best way to create a winning team is to put each player in the correct position based on his strengths. The same concept works in business. When employees "play the positions" on the team that match their strengths, they are happier and more productive. But more importantly, they see the talents each person contributes; the team as a whole is more cohesive and functions better.

Creating an environment where people with differing priorities are motivated to achieve excellence is possible, but it requires consistent planning, leadership and follow-up. Getting everyone to work together is not an easy task; but one of the greatest rewards of management is leading a diverse group of people toward the successful achievement of a common goal. Value your team's diversity. Then, manage each person as the unique and valuable asset they are.

Your difficult job is to manage each person as the unique and valuable asset they are.

Myths and Realities Summary

Myth	Reality
I will have more freedom to do what I want to do.	Greater responsibility usually means less freedom.
I will make more money.	Initially, you may make less money in exchange for added responsibility.
People will naturally follow me.	People will follow you only when you have earned their trust and respect.
I can change things quickly.	The timing of change is just as important as the change itself.
Everybody's performance can be turned around.	Somewhere along the way, you will have to de-hire someone.
I will be successful because I am in touch with my people.	You will be successful if you learn how to connect with your people.
It's easy to get everyone to work together.	Each person must be managed as the unique and valuable asset they are.

Why Managers Fail...

And What You Can Do To Succeed

Fear of failure is the greatest fear for most managers (or for most people, for that matter). And who can blame them? No one enjoys failing at anything.

Fear is an interesting thing. Sometimes, a little bit of fear can be a great motivator. But most of the time, fear is the thing that keeps us from achieving greatness. It stifles our creativity, prevents authentic communication, inhibits accountability and initiative, and stops us from taking the risks often required to do the right thing.

Many managers mistakenly believe the way to deal with this fear of failure is to ignore it – to shove it under the rug and pretend it isn't there. In fact, the opposite is true: The best way to attack any fear is to recognize and acknowledge it, understand as much as you can about it, and then develop a plan to address it.

Consequently, it is well worth your time to learn as much as you can about management failure. If you will study the reasons why managers fail, you can learn from those failures and take action to prevent them from happening to you. As the old saying goes, "Only a fool learns from his own mistakes; a wise man from the mistakes of others."

Many times it is just as profitable to learn from failure as it is to emulate success. Think of all the people you've worked for, beginning with your first part-time summer job. You can probably spot the potential management successes as well as the failures. If they were excellent leaders, you may have adopted parts of their work style as your own. If they were not effective managers, thank them anyway, because they taught you how NOT to manage…perhaps by painful example.

In this section, we will learn from the experiences of successful and not-so-successful managers. First, we'll take a look at the six most common causes of management failure and outline specific steps you can take to avoid the same pitfalls. But there's more to success than merely avoiding failure. You also have to know the right things to do and then do them. So, we'll uncover strategies, practices and attributes of successful managers that you can implement for yourself. Understand, these are not quick fixes, but habits you must cultivate over time if you intend to be successful in your role as a manager.

"Failure is, in a sense, the highway to success, as each discovery of what is false leads us to seek earnestly after what is true."

– John Keats

Managers Fail When They Lose Integrity and Trust

Failure

Whom do you trust?

Stop right now and make a list of five individuals you consider to be trustworthy. They may be family members, friends, business associates, or community leaders – it can be anyone as long as you trust them. Now look at your list and ask yourself, "What characteristics do these people have in common?" One trait they likely share is that you perceive them to be people who are honest and have integrity.

Now, make a list of five people you don't trust. What traits do these individuals share? You probably think of them as being dishonest or perhaps you question their integrity.

Honesty, integrity and trust are inextricably linked. If people perceive you to be a person of integrity, over time, you will earn their trust. On the other hand, if people have any reason to question your integrity, they will never trust you.

Recently, we have witnessed the public downfall of leaders from almost every walk of life – business, politics, non-profit organizations, sports, and even religion. We've watched – with the media and the world – as these people have earned prison sentences, lost their families, seen their wealth evaporate, and been stripped of every bit of dignity…all because they stepped over the integrity line.

In most cases, the root cause of these failures was that ego and pride took precedent over honesty and integrity. And, more than likely, it wasn't one isolated incident that caused these leaders' downfalls. People often lose integrity a little bit at a time and without realizing it.

Unfortunately, some leaders spend more time polishing their image than protecting their integrity. They're more concerned about how they look or sound than about their actions. But leaders will ultimately be judged on their actions, not their image.

These integrity failures are easy to criticize because they're newsworthy and involve high-profile people. However, thousands of managers have integrity failures and lose their employees' trust every day; and yet it never hits the news. But the effects of these integrity failures are just as devastating as the ones that make the headlines. Every time a manager steps over the integrity line, there is a direct negative impact on him/herself, the team, and the organization.

When managers lose the trust of their teams – or if they never had it to begin with – failure is imminent. Without trust, very little that a manager says or does will matter. Does it matter how often or how well you communicate with your people if they don't believe what you're saying? Does it matter how committed you are or what mission statement you have framed on the wall if your team doesn't trust you? Does it matter how optimistic you are, how skilled you are at resolving conflicts, or how courageous you are, if your team thinks you lack integrity?

The answer is "No." You can have all of these important leadership characteristics and still fail if your team doesn't trust you. When employees don't trust their manager, productivity, job satisfaction, morale, turnover and organizational pride are all negatively affected.

The importance of trust is so obvious…yet the breakdown of trust is still one of the leading causes of management failure. Without trust, you can effectively complete all the daily activities of a manager and still not achieve the results you want.

A manager's integrity and trust will be tested every day in both big and small ways. Managers who fail the integrity test will suffer great consequences. Those who pass will stay on the path toward success.

> *"Each time you are honest and conduct yourself with honesty, a success force will drive you toward greater success. Each time you lie, even a little white lie, there are strong forces pushing you toward failure."*
> — Joseph Sugarman

Success

Are *you* trustworthy?

Of course, all of us would like to think we are. But have we really earned our employees' trust? (Answer honestly!) If you're not sure you like your answer, that's okay. We're all human; we're not perfect. But we can, and should, strive to be better, to be more trustworthy.

Building and sustaining team and individual motivation requires a manager to earn the trust of every person they lead. If asked, the people on your team will most likely tell you it's most important to them that you are honest, trustworthy and that your words are in sync with your actions.

Unfortunately, your team won't necessarily trust you just because you're a good person. As a manager, you earn your employees' trust by consistently demonstrating integrity and honesty. Integrity is the commitment to do what is right regardless of the circumstances – no hidden agendas, no political games. Do the right thing, period.

Managers often mistakenly believe that trust is developed through the "big" things they do right. So it's easy to justify to themselves that it's no big deal if they compromise or bend the rules on a minor issue here and there. But your team holds you to a standard of absolute integrity on everything you do – big and small.

Trust is earned over time by doing many things right. As unfair as it may be, **earning trust sometimes takes years, but it can be destroyed in seconds by one simple action.** And in some cases, once it's destroyed, you can never earn it back again.

Effective managers know that trust is a critical factor in their success. Focus on building trust by focusing on your integrity. Here are some key action steps you can take to enhance your integrity:

♦ Establish integrity as your top priority. It should be the cornerstone of all your actions and decisions.

♦ Never compromise your integrity by rationalizing a situation as an "isolated incident." People are watching everything you do – there are no "isolated incidents." Firmly decide where your boundaries are, communicate those boundaries, and then stay within them.

♦ Never allow achieving results to become more important than the means to their achievement. For long-term sustained results, how you win is just as important as winning.

For greater success as a manager, maintain your integrity and continue to earn employees' trust by continually asking yourself these three questions:

1. Are integrity and trust my highest priorities? Do I subject my life and work to the highest scrutiny each and every day?

2. Are there areas of conflict between what I believe, what I say and how I behave?

3. Has compromise crept into my day-to-day life "under the radar"?

Protect your integrity like a priceless gem; it is your most precious management possession.

If you take care of your integrity,

your team's trust in you

will be sustained through the trials

of difficult management decisions.

Managers Fail Because They Do Not Clearly Communicate

Failure

There was a time, not so long ago, when lack of communication was a significant issue. But that is no longer the case – in today's tightly connected telecom/Internet world, the amount of communication is overwhelming. The number and type of communication methods alone is astounding – e-mail, voicemail, cellular phones, coast-to-coast walkie-talkies, pagers, video conferences, intranets...the list goes on and on.

With so much communication out there, it's hard to imagine it could be a problem – especially when one considers how much emphasis has been placed on communication in the workplace. Yet in almost every survey conducted within organizations, communication continues to be the number one frustration for employees. How can that be?

Although new tools like voicemail and e-mail have made communication easier, they have also de-personalized it. Modern managers can "communicate" with members of the team all day long without ever speaking to them. But chances are these managers haven't connected with anyone.

Another reason is that most managers have an inflated view of their ability to communicate effectively. One study revealed that 90% of managers believe their communication skills are in the top 10% of all managers. That means that 80% of these managers think they're

better communicators than they actually are. It's no wonder
communication is a key reason for management failure.

Then there are the managers who fall into the "clairvoyance trap" and
communicate little, if at all, with their employees. (Clairvoyance is the
ability to perceive things beyond the range of ordinary perception.)
These leaders believe their team members are clairvoyant – that they
know what to do without being told and can somehow automatically
sense what their roles and goals should be. These managers are easily
identified by their team members, who can frequently be heard saying,
"What was that all about? Does he expect us to read his mind?"

The communication problem is primarily one of quality, not quantity.
What is missing in most business communication today is human
understanding and connection. Managers often don't take the time
to ensure that what is being communicated is (1) relevant and
(2) understood.

If your team doesn't clearly and precisely understand your
communication, you will be constantly fighting an uphill battle in
your attempts to deliver results. Team members will lack direction
and motivation. Projects will fall behind schedule. People will lose
sight of the team's priorities.

A manager's ability to communicate effectively can make or break a
team and even an entire organization. A determining factor of a
manager's failure or success is not the strategy, but how well that strategy
is communicated and executed. Many great plans (and the managers
who championed them) have failed because of communication
breakdowns within an organization.

"Nothing is so simple that it cannot be misunderstood."
– Jr. Teague

Success

Communicating is the one thing we do more than anything else. But unfortunately, it's also typically the one thing we do less effectively than anything else. Crystal clear communication is a vital success tool for any manager. So what can you do to become a more capable communicator?

First, realize your team has an inherent need, and right, to know certain information. Most employees will tell you their information needs are relatively simple. They just want answers to the following questions:

♦ What is required of me? (Focus and Direction)

♦ What is in it for me? (Rewards)

♦ How am I doing? (Feedback)

Are you fulfilling your team members' need for information, or have you fallen into the clairvoyance trap? Remember that the people you work with are not "all knowing." Make it your priority for each team member to clearly understand the basics:

♦ Where the company/department/team is going.

♦ How the company/department/team is doing.

♦ Why their role is important.

♦ The performance you expect from them.

♦ How you will help them succeed.

Second, think of communication as a result as opposed to an activity. Pay more attention to **what** you communicate than **how** you communicate. Many managers get so caught up in the method (i.e, 3-D graphics, slick presentations), they lose sight of the message. Outcome-focused communication is crystal clear communication.

One way you can focus on the message is to make certain your communication is **relevant**. It has been estimated that 80 - 90% of all the communication we receive is not relevant to anything we do or anything we are working on. Getting rid of extraneous and unnecessary information allows people to concentrate on the essential news.

Finally, great leaders know that effective communication is as much about listening as it is talking. Communication is supposed to be a two-way process – where both parties give and both parties receive. It's not enough to just tell your team about a new organizational initiative. You have to follow up and listen to what they say so you can be certain the message you gave was the same one they received.

For greater success as a manager, eliminate the "static" in your communication by continually asking yourself these three questions:

1. Am I meeting each individual's need for information?

2. What is my desired outcome for this message – what do I want employees to think, feel and do after receiving it?

3. Am I listening to my team?

When managers are absolutely clear about what they want to communicate, and then connect with employees, they build commitment, passion and enthusiasm.

Communication is a two-way process.

Managers Fail Because They Lack Focus

Failure

One of the principal reasons for management failure and a great source of stress within most workgroups is a lack of focus. Lack of focus wreaks havoc on a team and an organization; it reduces team members' trust in their leader and limits a manager's ability to deliver results on a daily basis.

Certainly there are many external factors that make it difficult for teams to focus on priorities. Business today is very complex. And the more complex things are, the easier it is to lose focus. But without a doubt, the biggest cause of complexity and lack of focus in the workplace is management. That's right – as a manager, you have the ability to create mammoth complexity or beautiful simplicity for your team.

Creating and maintaining focus for the team could very well be the most critical aspect of a manager's job; it's definitely the most challenging one. Managers are in a difficult situation. Today's environment requires flexible organizations, ready to adapt to changing market conditions. But constant changes and distractions cause us to jump from one activity to another and then another, often not finishing any of them.

When managers don't maintain their focus, and therefore the team's focus, the team lacks direction and clarity. Employees don't know where to aim, where to direct their energy and attention. Confusion and complexity increase. People don't see how what they do ties to the big picture, and it's difficult to keep everyone on the team headed in the same direction. If the team hits the target and achieves its goal – and that's a big "if" – it will be because of luck and not because the manager did a great job leading the team.

Lack of focus is a huge de-motivator for employees. It creates situations in which things that are normally simple become very complex and in which people easily lose perspective. Team members are never quite sure what the priorities are or what to work on next. And why should they bother anyway – the priority will probably just change again tomorrow.

When managers lack focus, their teams lack focus. When teams lack focus, they can't consistently produce results. And when teams don't produce results, managers fail!

"The successful person is the average person, focused."
– Unknown

Success

When it comes to focus, you can be the problem or you can be the solution – it's your choice. As a leader, it's your responsibility to manage the complexities your team faces and create focus where there is none.

Granted, you can't control everything that happens within your department or on your team. But you can manage those items and issues within your realm of control. Your team should never have to second-guess you, question the team's priorities, wonder what they should be working on, or spend time figuring out what to do next.

"Focus" is defined as "directing energy toward a particular point or purpose." The most critical management decision you will make is to determine what is the most important thing for you and your team. We call it the "main thing" – the one point or purpose toward which your team should be directing its energy and attention. If you and your team were able to accomplish only one thing, what would that be?

Do you know what your main thing is? If you don't, we'll guarantee your team doesn't either. But even if you do, we'd be willing to bet that every member of your team doesn't know what the main thing is. Don't believe us? Go ask them. More than likely, you'll get a variety of different answers.

You need to know what your main thing is. Your team needs to know what the main thing is. Without it, everyone will be focused on different outcomes. Great leaders understand the value of knowing their main thing. They realize that to keep their teams focused, they must simplify complex situations into a single, organizing idea – the kind of basic principle that unifies, organizes, and guides all decisions.

Set aside a time to get together and, as a team, decide what your main thing is. Your main thing should answer the question, "Why are we here?" or "What is our purpose?" Here are some examples from other teams:

♦ We provide outstanding customer service.

♦ We produce defect-free products.

♦ We develop customized solutions for our customers.

♦ We meet the needs of the departments we serve.

As the manager, you must also make a commitment to determine and focus on your personal main thing. The truth is, it's usually the manager who is constantly changing the team's direction and focus. If your main thing is always changing, expect nothing but frustrated employees. If you're focused on your main thing, your team will naturally be focused on their main thing.

Determining the main thing is actually the easy part. The hard part is ensuring you and your team stay focused on the main thing. Start by constantly reinforcing what the main thing is until you're absolutely certain everyone clearly understands it. You should be able to ask any team member at any time, "What's our main thing?" and consistently get the same answer.

Next, you must develop the plans, processes, and action items that represent the steps necessary to accomplish the main thing. This information must be communicated to, and clearly understood by, every member of the team.

Finally, identify and eliminate any unnecessary activities that don't support your main thing or that block the progress and success of your people. Test all of the team's decisions and activities against the main thing. Then have the courage to stop doing the things that distract the team from accomplishing its number one priority.

For greater success as a manager, stay focused by continually asking yourself these three questions:

1. What is our team's main thing and why?

2. Do we test all of our actions and decisions against our main thing?

3. Do I create distractions and confusion for my team, or do I allow everyone to focus on accomplishing the main thing?

Laser sharp focus is not something that is natural or easy. Without question, you will face distractions that will tend to pull you away from your main thing. That's okay. Your job is to continually reinforce and communicate the main thing, hone your focus, and keep the team on track. That will ensure your team's success – and yours as well.

Keep the main thing the main thing.

Managers Fail When They Ignore Problems

Failure

Wouldn't it be great if every morning when we woke up, all the problems we had the previous day were gone? Life sure would be a lot easier! Unfortunately, it rarely works that way.

Problems, and the conflict that often comes with them, are unavoidable – especially in the workplace. As long as people have to work together 40 hours a week, there will always be problems and conflict.

There's an interesting dynamic that occurs with how people react to problems. When a problem affects us personally, we usually want it fixed immediately! But if we're not directly affected, most of us would rather do almost anything than deal with a problem. For most people, it's natural to want to avoid conflict.

But managers who consistently avoid problems and ignore conflicts are putting their jobs in jeopardy. Perhaps these managers are overwhelmed with other priorities and don't see a problem as something that needs their immediate attention. Other managers believe that if an issue doesn't directly involve them, employees should be left to resolve problems on their own. Or maybe some managers simply aren't sure how to solve a problem, and so they do nothing, thinking that if they ignore the issue long enough it will go away on its own.

But in most cases, problems don't just go away. In fact, the longer a disruptive situation continues, the more expensive and painful it will be to solve. Avoiding problems invariably creates even bigger problems.

The 1-10-100 Rule illustrates the impact of allowing problems to persist. This rule states that a conflict addressed quickly and efficiently can be solved with the equivalent of one (1) unit of time, money or resources. If the problem is not addressed immediately, it grows and expands. At this point, it will take the equivalent of ten (10) units of time, money or resources to solve. And if the problem lingers even longer, it will likely spread to other people, processes, departments or customers. Now it will require the equivalent of at least one hundred (100) units of time, money, or resources to resolve. That's one hundred times what it would have cost to solve the exact same problem in the beginning. A problem that could have been solved at the outset by focusing on it for 30 minutes, could eventually take over a week of someone's time to sort out and fix. The long-term implications of avoiding just a few minor problems on your team can be devastating.

Even managers who do attempt to handle conflicts quickly frequently fail because they mandate a solution based solely on their perceptions of the situation. These managers tend to place minimal value on the views and expertise of others. They make isolated decisions because they don't take the time to listen to those involved, get the facts, ask questions, and investigate. The best managers solve problems by listening to others...failing managers already know all the answers.

When it comes to problems and conflict, managers who bury their heads in the sand will find their backsides are exposed!

> *"The significant problems we face today cannot be solved at the same level of thinking we were at when we created them."*
>
> – Albert Einstein

Success

In order to be successful, a manager has no alternative but to address problems. In fact, it is every manager's job to make sure problems are solved before they become an emergency (and cost the organization one hundred times more than they should have). The real question is, how big of a role should a manager play in solving problems and conflicts?

Should you lead your team by the hand? Should you serve as the "point person," steering the team around land mines and away from sniper fire? You certainly can choose to play the lead role in solving your team's problems; but you may soon find you've become a convenient corporate dumping ground for every colleague's issues and problems.

Said one president, "My job is to solve the problems my team members cannot."

Are most managers really that smart...that they can find solutions to problems that the entire team together could not resolve? Occasionally that may be the case – there are definitely those issues that you, and only you, are qualified or responsible for solving. But it's rare that a team can't solve a problem *if* it's given the authority to do so and is taught problem-solving skills.

The manager's role is to facilitate a process for the team to identify, develop and then implement acceptable solutions to its problems. The key to success is to teach team members how to use the process so they can follow it themselves.

An effective problem-solving process involves four steps:

Step 1. Define the problem in writing. Stating the issue on paper clarifies the situation. You can't discuss possible solutions until everyone clearly understands what the problem is. Make sure the following questions are answered: *What is the current situation? What is the impact of this problem? What is the desired end-state?* As the team addresses these questions, encourage everyone to stick to the facts and leave emotions out of the discussion. Everyone has to agree on the answers to these three questions before moving to the next step.

Step 2. Consider potential solutions. Involve people in the problem-solving process by brainstorming various alternatives. Solicit input from the members of your team, your manager, and, depending on the issue, even your customers. Other people are your best source of information. Gain their feedback and insights, use their ideas, and let them participate in the discussion and planning. The key is to listen. Asking without listening produces cynicism and creates obstacles to the process.

Step 3. Identify the best solution. Evaluate all the possibilities uncovered in Step 2. To do that, you'll need to gather more information: *Are all of the potential solutions doable? What is the impact of each option? What will be required in order to implement each option?* Now you can develop a workable solution based on input and involvement from others as well as your own experience. You have completed this step when you have identified a solution that will solve all, or almost all, of the problem for good. (Don't skip this step! If you do, you'll end up with a "shotgun approach" where multiple solutions are implemented without thinking through the impact of those solutions. You may solve the problem in the short term, but create bigger problems long term because you didn't consider the downstream implications.)

Step 4. Implement and communicate the plan and then monitor results. Involve the team in developing a plan to implement and communicate the solution, including additional areas for improvement and newly discovered opportunities. Then track progress to ensure the problem is solved. (This should be the easiest step in the process if the other three steps were done properly.)

As you may remember from your days as an individual contributor, management decisions are almost always questioned. (Surprise! This now includes your decisions. Yes, your decisions will be "Monday-morning quarterbacked" at the water fountain, in the lunchroom and in countless e-mails.)

But when employees are the key contributors in the problem-solving process – with you as the facilitator – the decisions are rarely second-guessed. Consistent team involvement gives people a sense of pride and ownership of both the problem and the solution. And, it dramatically increases commitment to the solution, to you as a leader, and ultimately to the organization.

For greater success as a manager, help your team solve its problems by continually asking yourself these three questions:

1. Have I trained my team in a systematic way to solve problems?

2. Do I set the example for my team by being a good listener?

3. What impact will the solution have on my team, our organization and our clients?

We've already acknowledged that problem solving is not easy. Remember that management is often a balancing act. You must always walk the fine line of knowing when and how far to insert yourself into any given situation. If your team is properly trained on how to solve problems, your intervention will be required less often.

Teach your team how to effectively

solve problems for themselves.

Then be a facilitator and cheerleader.

Managers Fail Because They Hire the Wrong People

Failure

Many managers fail because they don't realize their hiring decisions are more important than their management process. You can have the best management process around, but if you have the wrong people on the team, your chances for success are slim and none.

Ever heard the well-worn comment, "This company's greatest assets are its people"? The business gurus have decided it simply isn't true. Only the RIGHT people are an organization's greatest assets. And as a manager, your greatest liability is having the wrong people on your team.

A manager's job is difficult enough to begin with; it becomes next to impossible when the manager has to spend all of his or her time and attention on "people issues" that drive no value. Having the wrong people on the team drags the entire team down and makes it even more challenging to consistently deliver results.

Hiring the right people is not easy, and the reality is that the vast majority of managers are not trained in or skilled at interviewing. And it does take skill, practice and patience. But most managers hire fewer than five people a year. How good can you be at a process you complete so infrequently? Thomas Jefferson wrote to John Adams in a letter in 1823: "No duty the executive has to perform is so trying as to put the right person in the right place." The same thing holds true today.

The enemy of getting the right person in the right job is time. Managers are faced with the decision to either maintain an open position or hire someone who is not qualified to fill that position. It's a tough call. Many managers succumb to the pressure of "I have to have a warm body *now*." They quickly discover that the short-term relief of filling the position is overtaken by the long-term pain of having hired the wrong person. Don't compromise to fill a position; you will pay for it later.

Many managers think they can solve the problem of finding qualified candidates and quickly fill a position by hiring from within the organization. But that's not always a good solution either.

A manager in a company we worked with was desperate to fill a customer service supervisory position. She had a team member with extraordinary customer service talent, so she promoted her. "She had the right skills and was very genuine and empathetic when she worked with customers," the manager said.

However, in a management role, this same empathetic, sensitive individual became very directive and demanding. She required each team member to do things exactly the way she had done her job because that was how she had achieved success. Within a few months, it was obvious she was managing her team into the ground. This once star performer didn't last 90 days.

The bottom line is this: A mistake in the hiring process is one of the costliest mistakes a manager can make. Not having the right people on the team robs you of your greatest performance leverage.

"If you want to make a silk purse out of a sow's ear, it helps to start with a silk sow."
– Steve Ventura

Success

As a manager, your ability to surround yourself with extraordinary talent is not just a necessary part of your job, it's critical to your success! Quickly identifying the right talent is a delicate blend of art and science. There is, and always will be, much debate about how to evaluate prospective job candidates.

On one side of the debate are industrial psychologists who have developed scores of assessments, from skills-based inventories to personality profiling and traditional IQ testing. On the face of it, most assessments are valid and useful instruments with reams of research to back their results. However, if you elect to rely solely on the results of assessments to select candidates, you could knock out very qualified, very dynamic talent.

On the other side of the debate are individuals who claim they can spot good talent anywhere and rely solely on their "gut instincts" during interviews. There's no question there's value to subjective judgment and intuition in the hiring process. But again, if you rely only on instinct, you may be as successful at finding the right person as a fortuneteller who claims to "see" the future in a crystal ball.

The best answer is to use a combination of assessment and intuition, because both have a role in the hiring process.

Here are a few tips to help you find the right people for your team:

♦ When interviewing candidates, use the 3 Rules of 3:

• Interview at least 3 qualified candidates for each position;

• Interview each candidate at least 3 times; and

• Have 3 team members evaluate each candidate.

♦ Interview candidates at different times during the day – for example, in the early morning one time and in the afternoon another time. You're hiring them to work all day long; it might be wise to see how they perform at different times of the day.

♦ Have an interview tract or outline established before the interview. This ensures that you will ask each candidate the same questions in the same order. It allows you to concentrate on the candidates' responses and evaluate what they're saying, instead of worrying about what your next question will be.

♦ Actively search for candidates who have different skills and qualities than you. Sociological studies show that most managers tend to hire people just like themselves. But this limits the possibility for a diverse group of individuals who bring a variety of skills and talents to the table and are therefore better able to deliver results.

Perhaps the most important piece of advice we can give you about the hiring process is to get some help from hiring experts. Seek the help of your Human Resources department for legal issues, interviewing tips, lists of interview questions, etc. There are also numerous books available on the subject of interviewing skills and techniques. Successful managers don't necessarily need to have excellent interviewing skills – they just need to know where to go for help when the time comes.

Take your time and find the most talented people for the job. Your new employees must be competent enough to reach their desired level of productivity quickly and fit in well enough to remain with the organization long enough to recoup the cost of hiring them. Do it slowly; do it well.

For greater success as a manager, find the best people for your open positions by continually asking yourself these three questions:

1. Am I utilizing all the resources available to me to hire the right person?

2. Am I taking my time to find the best person who will benefit our team?

3. Does this person fit into our culture and have the necessary technical skills?

When you have an open position, look upon that challenge as a great opportunity. You have the ability to make a tremendous difference in your team and your success. Your goal should be to hire tough and manage easy.

Having the right people on your team

is the leverage you need for greater success.

Managers Fail Because They Refuse to Leave The Comfort Zone

Failure

Managers who choose to rest on their knowledge and who are not committed to improvement are doomed to fail. It's that simple – there's no other way to put it. In today's fast-paced and constantly changing global economy, managers who aren't growing are falling behind their peers in terms of skills, knowledge and experience.

These managers fail to realize that complacency is the root of mediocrity. They get stuck in the "comfort zone" and don't know how to get out. The comfort zone is a place where people are so accustomed to their situation, surroundings, and skills that any change – even one for the better – is resisted. **The comfort zone is full of people who refuse to invest time and energy in personal improvement and so are passed by others who make personal improvement a priority.**

Successful managers know what average managers do not: The comfort zone is the number one obstacle to fulfilling your potential.

> *"If you employed study, thinking, and planning time daily, you could develop and use the power that can change the course of your destiny."*
>
> – W. Clement Stone

Success

If you desire long-term success – whether it's success in your professional or personal life – you've got to get out of the comfort zone and commit to being in a life-long learning zone. The pain of lost opportunity lasts far longer than the pleasure of today's laziness. Don't miss your chance.

The good news is that you have the power right now to make changes that will prepare you for future success. What kind of changes would you like to make? What areas or skills can you improve that would further your career (or just get you back up to speed)? Now, take action!

First, set some specific goals for improvement. Don't just talk about improvement, get on with it. Talk is cheap. Set your goals and develop a plan to make them happen. Most people today don't even have goals. How can you expect improvement if you don't know what you want to accomplish? Success is rehearsed long before it "suddenly appears," and the rehearsal begins with setting specific goals. (There are lots of resources available to help you with goal setting – check online or visit your local bookstore.)

Second, read more. Readers are leaders. The more you learn, the more you will earn. Did you know you could be in the top 1% of all readers by reading just one book a month? A book a month is roughly the equivalent of half a chapter a day – just 10 to 15 minutes. What an incredible return on your investment. Imagine the incredible amount of knowledge and wisdom you'll discover.

Third, teach others who are interested. When you find something you like – pass it on! The wealth of knowledge and ideas that can be brought forth and shared is incredible. It's been documented that teams flourish in an environment of learning, innovation and creativity. So provide a foundation of learning for your people – promote books, distribute articles, attend conferences, and share the learning. As you teach others, you hone and update your own skills. Give your knowledge away, and you will become more knowledgeable.

For greater success as a manager, get out of the comfort zone by continually asking yourself these three questions:

1. Do I have goals and are they clearly defined?
2. Do I read at least ten minutes a day about how I can become a better manager or person?
3. Do I promote an environment of learning and creativity for my team?

Live and promote a life of learning!

**Get out of the comfort zone
and into the learning zone.**

Failure and Success Summary

Failure	Success
Managers fail when they lose integrity and trust.	If you take care of your integrity, your team's trust in you will be sustained through the trials of difficult management decisions.
Managers fail because they don't clearly communicate.	Communication is a two-way process.
Managers fail because they lack focus.	Keep the main thing the main thing.
Managers fail when they ignore problems.	Teach your team how to effectively solve problems for themselves.
Managers fail because they hire the wrong people.	Having the right people on your team is the leverage you need for greater success.
Managers fail because they refuse to leave the comfort zone.	Get out of the comfort zone and into the learning zone.

Success or Failure...

Which Do You Choose?

Management is not for the faint of heart. A career in management holds awesome responsibilities accompanied by the consequences of failure that can be far reaching. There are few jobs that provide a person with the opportunity to have a huge impact on the corporate bottom line by achieving results through the guidance and direction of others.

A career in management offers daily challenges and tremendous rewards. Managers can challenge themselves as well as help the people they lead reach goals and achieve success.

Consider the managers you've had in the past and the positive impact they've had on your life and career. You now have that same opportunity to make a difference for the people you manage. The bonuses of successful management extend well beyond any financial rewards. While money is important, the true prize lies in the personal satisfaction of providing an environment in which others may grow and develop.

Challenge yourself to dig deep into the role of a manager. Practice the truths and dispel the myths of management. Read all you can about leadership and management and become a life-long learner who strives to keep their skills fresh and their attitude positive. Learn and apply new skills that will not only accelerate your growth and success, but the growth and success of your people as well.

Begin to know those points of weakness all of us have and take steps to keep them from derailing your success. Management failure is devastating to all, and in today's business environment, the stakes are even higher. There is more pressure to produce results, and the scrutiny and distrust of management is at an all time high.

Take advantage of the past mistakes and experiences of managers and leaders that have gone before you. At the same time, associate with and learn from those highly successful managers who know what it takes to produce results through others.

We hope this book has provided you with insights into what it takes to become, and remain, a successful manager. As you've discovered, management success is based on your ability to produce tangible results through other people while positively impacting their lives. You can now avoid the traps, mistakes and failures of others and get on with the incredibly rewarding experience of being a leader.

Never forget – management is the opportunity of a lifetime for those who choose to accept the responsibilities. May life's journey bring you success, happiness, balance to your life, and a clear vision of the opportunities presented to you!

"We all leave footprints in the sand.
The question is, will we be a big heel,
or a great soul?"
– Unknown

Personal Insights…

From Successful Managers

Who: **Paul Brochu**
Organization: **Valero LP**
Title: **Vice President –**
Corporate Development
Years in Leadership: **22**

What myths had you heard about management that you later found to be untrue?
Once you become a manager, you've "made it." Actually, managers are more vulnerable. Think about it: When a sports team isn't winning, the players don't get fired, the coach does. Managers are coaches. It's the manager who takes the heat for results that are below expectations.

What realities of management did you face that you were not fully prepared for?
Your workload increases no matter how well you can delegate.

What are the most common mistakes managers make that can lead to failure?
Managing everyone at all times with one style of management. Good managers understand the need for, and effectiveness of, situational leadership. Knowing when and how to apply the different styles will enhance your managerial competence.

What are the critical factors necessary for management success?
The desire and ability to continue to learn. There is danger in the status quo. Leaders always learn and learners always lead. Good managers will always seek to improve their skill sets and learn from their mistakes. Managers haven't "made it," they have only begun to learn what it takes to successfully run an organization of complex elements called people.

Who: **Norman Schippers**
Organization: **Hewitt Associates**
Title: **North American Talent and**
Organizational Consulting Leader
Years in Leadership: **10**

What myths had you heard about management that you later found to be untrue?
Changes you initiate as a manager happen more quickly and effectively than changes initiated as an individual contributor. The reality is that being one step removed from the field or client actually causes change to happen more slowly.

What realities of management did you face that you were not fully prepared for?
The impact and implications of my decisions. Ideas or changes that I might enact in my area many times have far-reaching impact (cascading effect) on other areas of the business.

What are the most common mistakes managers make that can lead to failure?
Thinking that everyone will embrace and love change and can see the vision as clearly as you can. While you as a manager might be focused on the end of the race, the people you are leading are still at the starting line.

What are the critical factors necessary for management success?
Build credibility and find quick small wins to establish your foundation for success. Understand where the informal power is – title alone does not always signify where the true power lies, and a miscalculation in this area can mean disaster.

Who: **Martha Thomas**
Organization: **SchlumbergerSema**
Title: **Vice President – Network and**
Infrastructure Solutions, N. America
Years in Leadership: **12**

What myths had you heard about management that you later found to be untrue?
The manager is the sole decision maker. I found the majority of decisions are made either in a team environment or require some type of collaboration and buy-in to be effective.

What realities of management did you face that you were not fully prepared for?
Your credibility will be questioned – so stick to your guns!

What are the most common mistakes managers make that can lead to failure?
Forgetting the hard work, sacrifices and respect that landed you the management position. Never forget what made you successful.

What are the critical factors necessary for management success?
Good communication skills – both upward and downward in the organization.

Who: **Pete Silewicz**

Organization: **Loomis Fargo**

Title: **Senior Vice President**

Years in Leadership: **25**

What myths had you heard about management that you later found to be untrue?
Because you are a manager, you will have followers. True, but committed followers come only after you gain their trust – which needs to be renewed daily.

What realities of management did you face that you were not fully prepared for?
Accepting full responsibility for others' actions and results. Making the difficult hiring and firing decisions that are necessary for a sustained, high-performance team. As a manager, you must remain objective in setting expectations and in your evaluation of performance results.

What are the most common mistakes managers make that can lead to failure?
The notion that I, the manager, must do it all. In part, it's a time management dilemma; and in other ways it's a question of what are my job and goals.

What are the critical factors necessary for management success?
Good people skills. Treating people with respect – if you choose to manage from a position of authority all the time, you will fail. Listening skills – the kind of listening where you lean in and really absorb what someone is trying to tell you and then provide feedback.

Who: **Larry Goodwin**

Organization: **Continental Airlines**

Title: **Vice President – Reservations**

Years in Leadership: **28**

What myths had you heard about management that you later found to be untrue?
Experienced managers don't have to work as hard as new managers.

What realities of management did you face that you were not fully prepared for?
Leadership requires that you make a personal connection at some level with the people you lead.

What are the most common mistakes managers make that can lead to failure?
Trying to please everyone and be everyone's friend.

What are the critical factors necessary for management success?
The ability to quickly think on your feet.

Who: **Pat Carroll**

Organization: **Fujitsu Consulting**

Title: **Vice President**

Years in Leadership: **25**

What myths had you heard about management that you later found to be untrue?
A manager can do the job at their "normal course and speed." A management position usually requires more time and energy and is a more stressful assignment.

What realities of management did you face that you were not fully prepared for?
The increased pressure from above for results and performance.

What are the most common mistakes managers make that can lead to failure?
Many managers get carried away with the power they perceive they have once they're in management – they fail to listen, learn, and collaborate. Ultimately, a manager needs the support and performance of the team to be successful.

What are the critical factors necessary for management success?
A strong level of self-confidence, self-control, and empathy.

About the Authors

Ken Carnes is Managing Director of Aristevo Performance Consulting, an internationally known organization that focuses on developing high potential sales and leadership talent. He has over 20 years of domestic and international sales, training and executive management experience, including senior positions with FedEx, AchieveGlobal and Provant. He was also President of The Ransford Group, an influential consulting firm focused on providing talent, training and strategy to the consulting industry. With Aristevo, Ken works with some of the world's most respected organizations, such as Hewlett Packard, Schlumberger and Hewitt Associates.

David Cottrell, President and CEO of CornerStone Leadership Institute, is an internationally known leadership consultant, educator and speaker. His business experience includes senior management positions with Xerox and FedEx. He also led the successful turnaround of a chapter eleven company before founding CornerStone. David's 25-plus years of professional experience are reflected in fifteen highly acclaimed books and his reputation as a premier public speaker.

Mark C. Layton is Chairman, President and CEO of PFSweb Inc. (NASDAQ: PFSW), a leading Business Process Outsourcing (BPO) Services provider. He is a recognized leader in the utilization of technology in business, and as such, is a highly sought public speaker on issues including electronic commerce, leadership, technology trends, supply chain management, web-enabled call centers, financial management and Christian business principles. Mark is the author of *.coms or .bombs: Strategies for Profit in e-Business* and co-author of *Listen Up, Customer Service* and *175 Ways to Get More Done In Less Time.*

Maximize the Management Insights *impact throughout your organization with these powerful turnkey tools!*

Management Insights 360° Profile

The *Management Insights* On-line Profile provides new managers, prospective management candidates or high potentials considering a career in management a quick and affordable, feedback mechanism that matches their own perceptions and other's (peers, managers and team members) against those attributes and competencies required to successfully manage people. Based on the best selling book *Management Insights*, individuals are profiled in following categories:

- ♦ Relationship Building
- ♦ Influence
- ♦ Business Perspective
- ♦ Analysis and Judgment
- ♦ Interpersonal Communications
- ♦ Conflict Resolution
- ♦ Initiating and Managing Change
- ♦ Creativity and Innovation
- ♦ Developing Self and Others

Management Insights Presentation Companion Piece

Enhance the *Management Insights* experience in your organization with this complete and cost effective companion presentation piece. All the main concepts and ideas in the book are summarized and outlined in this professionally produced PowerPoint presentation. Use the presentation for kickoff meetings, training sessions or as a follow-on reinforcement tool. When you order you will receive:

- ♦ Complete *Management Insights* PowerPoint Slide Deck
- ♦ Easy to Follow Facilitator Guide and Notes
- ♦ Participant Guide

Make the *Management Insights* experience come alive today!

Affordable: Only **$79.95**

Recommended Reading for Managers:

Monday Morning Leadership is David Cottrell's newest and best-selling book. It offers unique encouragement and direction that will help you become a better manager, employee, and person. **$12.95**
Monday Morning Leadership **Audio CD** **$19.95**

Manager's Communication Handbook is a powerful handbook that will help you connect with employees and create the understanding, support and acceptance critical to your success. It will introduce you to the four key dimensions of communication and teach you how to eliminate communication static. **$9.95**

The Manager's Coaching Handbook is a practical guide to improving performance from your superstars, middle stars and falling stars. **$9.95**

175 Ways to Get More Done in Less Time has 175 really, really good suggestions that will help you get things done faster…usually better. **$9.95**

Sticking To It: The Art of Adherence reveals the secrets to success for high-achieving individuals and teams. It offers practical steps to help you consistently executive your plans. Read it and WIN! **$9.95**

Nuts 'n Bolts provides practical, easy to follow "how to's" to help your people meet their most challenging leadership responsibilities. **$9.95**

Becoming the Obvious Choice is a roadmap showing each employee how they can maintain their motivation, develop their hidden talents, and become the best. **$9.95**

180 Ways to Walk the Recognition Talk is packed with proven techniques and practical strategies that will help you encourage positive, productive performance. **$9.95**

136 Effective Presentation Tips is a powerful handbook providing 136 practical, easy to use tips to make every presentation a success. **$9.95**

Listen Up, Leader! Ever wonder what employees think about their leaders? This book tells you the seven characteristics of leadership that people will follow. **$9.95**

NEW!! *Management Insights 360° Profile* To order, visit www.cornerstoneleadership.com **$99.95**

Visit www.**cornerstoneleadership**.com
for additional books and resources.

☑ YES! Please send me extra copies of *Management Insights*!
1-30 copies $14.95   31-100 copies $13.95   100+ copies $12.95

Management Insights	_____ copies X _____	= $ _____

Additional Leadership Development Books

Monday Morning Leadership	_____ copies X $12.95	= $ _____
Monday Morning Leadership Audio CD	_____ copies X $19.95	= $ _____
Manager's Communication Handbook	_____ copies X $9.95	= $ _____
The Manager's Coaching Handbook	_____ copies X $9.95	= $ _____
175 Ways to Get More Done in Less Time	_____ copies X $9.95	= $ _____
Sticking To It: The Art of Adherence	_____ copies X $9.95	= $ _____
Nuts 'n Bolts	_____ copies X $9.95	= $ _____
Becoming the Obvious Choice	_____ copies X $9.95	= $ _____
180 Ways to Walk the Recognition Talk	_____ copies X $9.95	= $ _____
136 Effective Presentation Tips	_____ copies X $9.95	= $ _____
Listen Up, Leader!	_____ copies X $9.95	= $ _____
Management Insight's Package (one of each of the 11 items above)	_____ packs X $119.95	= $ _____
	Shipping & Handling	$ _____
	Subtotal	$ _____
	Sales Tax (8.25%-TX Only)	$ _____
	Total (U.S. Dollars Only)	$ _____

Shipping and Handling Charges

Total $ Amount	Up to $50	$51-$99	$100-$249	$250-$1199	$1200-$3000	$3000+
Charge	$5	$8	$16	$30	$80	$125

Name _____ Job Title _____

Organization _____ Phone _____

Shipping Address _____ Fax _____

Billing Address _____ Email _____

City _____ State _____ Zip _____

❏ Please invoice (Orders over $200) Purchase Order Number (if applicable) _____

Charge Your Order: ❏ MasterCard   ❏ Visa   ❏ American Express

Credit Card Number _____ Exp. Date _____

Signature _____

❏ Check Enclosed (Payable to CornerStone Leadership)

Fax	**Mail**	**Phone**
972.274.2884	P.O. Box 764087 Dallas, TX 75376	888.789.5323

www.**cornerstoneleadership**.com